What People Are Saying

"Packed with highly actionable and practical advice. It's more than just a book for business, it's the unwritten rule book for living your best life."

Elaine Rau
CEO & Founder of LadyBossBlogger.com

"Success in life comes, in part, from knowing its unwritten rules. Whether you're a recent grad or a seasoned professional, *Nobody Told Me!* is for you. It pairs common sense wisdom with fresh thinking that can lead you to a new way of living and working."

Jennifer Large
Vice President, Talent Development & Workforce Impact, Fluor Corporation

"This guide to the unwritten rules could eliminate countless hours of frustration for new employees and managers. The action-focused instructions are a great way to set and meet expectations. What great reminders of how to present and represent yourself!"

Kate Maurin
Global Director of Talent, Alcoa Corporation

"Reading *Nobody Told Me!* should be a graduation requirement for every high school and university student. I recommend we all read this once a year for our own benefit and for the benefit of those around us."

Dave Van Drunen
Account Executive, Concurrency, Inc.

"Rose has put down on paper the words of wisdom we all wish we would have received earlier in our careers. And, these are good reminders for those of us who have been around the block. After reading this, you can Consider Yourself Told!"

Beth Gunderson
Founder, Minikahda Partners

"Every professional needs to know how to ensure that they do not trip over the minefields present in any organization. Rose has written *the* handbook that benefits not only new professionals, but also those with extensive experience. This is a book that I will be giving to many. I cannot recommend this book more highly!"

Marina Davis
Director, Organization and Talent Development, CBiz

"Rose has captured a practical yet comprehensive collection of the un-written rules of success. Her experience in large and small companies, academia and executive coaching give her a unique perspective on what's required for success. The wisdom she shares will serve any professional well."

Danae Atkins
Talent Development Director

"This wonderful book is absolutely amazing and absolutely necessary! The rules include actions we see in successful leaders, but could never quite put into words. I will be giving a copy of this practical, insightful guide to all of my emerging leaders and high-potential performers."

Bethanne Panos
SVP, Human Resources, Calamos Investments

NOBODY TOLD ME!

NOBODY TOLD ME!

129 Unwritten Rules for Career Success

Rose Hollister

Big Snowy
MEDIA

For information, contact:
Big Snowy Media
209 E. Liberty Drive
Wheaton IL 60187

Big Snowy Media edition published 2018.

....

Library of Congress Cataloging-in-Publication Data
Hollister, Lynda Jeanne, 1960—
Nobody Told Me: 129 Unwritten Rules for Career Success (Big Snowy Media)

Business and Self-Improvement

ISBN 978-0-692-14716-0

To Michael, Cameron, and Jessica—
My whole world begins and ends with you.

CONTENTS

INTRODUCTION

From Cornfields to Corporate . . .

I grew up in rural Ohio. Our house was surrounded by cornfields on every side. Looking back, I do not remember knowing anyone involved in a large company or in corporate America. The people I knew were farmers, housewives, teachers, laborers and university staff and faculty. Following a bachelor's, master's and five years of working in academe, I landed a consulting job with a small business in downtown Chicago. As I interacted with people in a wide variety of businesses and industries, I soon realized I had a lot to learn. Successful business people dressed, talked and behaved in a certain way. I watched. I listened. There seemed to be rules that most of the highly successful people were following.

Little by little, I learned the unwritten rules; they seemed to be the keys to success. These rules were not covered in my education or my reading. They were never in the policy manual or the employee handbook. The unwritten rules are the ones that no one tells you, however, they may have a huge impact on your career.

Many jobs later, while working as an executive and consultant at Fortune 500 companies, I realized that others might benefit from these unwritten rules. When I taught graduate students, it was clear they needed these rules as well. As a consultant and executive coach, I heard leaders echo the fact that their team members were missing a baseline of information.

Many people have never been exposed to these extensive but unwritten rules. Although they seem to be a part of the business marketplace, usually, these rules are not written down. Yet, not following these unwritten rules hurts business people every day. Paying attention to these elements can help people avoid the potential landmines that may hinder one's reputation and one's work. This book is my collection of the rules that I wish someone had given me early in my career.

These rules apply to many workplaces. The rules, for the most part, are fundamentals to make everyone's life easier. However, each organization has its own unique set of unwritten rules. For every company that follows the rule, "Be a team player," there may be another that says, "Be out for yourself and step on anyone who gets in your way."

This book offers a beginning set of rules to guide your behaviors and actions. Use them as a baseline; as you study your new workplace, assess your current culture against the rules in this book.

Not following the rules may hurt your performance, your reputation and your career. Choose at your own risk. It's OK not to play by the rules; just know that there may be consequences.

This book is like a bowl of popcorn. You can have one kernel, a handful or the whole bowl.

And, these are not the only rules.

Please add your rules to *Rule@RoseHollister.com*

Chapter One

ANTHROPOLOGY AT WORK

How to learn the unwritten rules.

To learn the unwritten rules, begin by being extraordinarily observant. Look around. What do people talk about most? What gets significant time and attention? What seems most important?

Act like an anthropologist in learning about your workplace. Some elements of culture, like dress, are easy to see. Others, like learning what matters most to your boss, will take some time to figure out.

1. FIGURE OUT THE "TIME LANGUAGE" AT YOUR PLACE OF EMPLOYMENT.

Time will have different definitions depending on your location.

A CASE IN POINT

At Jessica's first job, she knew that her colleagues were at their desks by 7:30 at the latest. When she moved to a new company, no one arrived before 9:30, but employees stayed much later.

At one company, a meeting is scheduled for 10 o'clock. The real meeting starts at 10:15. No one is present at 10 and then people wander in between 10 and 10:15. Coming in at 10:10 is considered coming in early. People socialize and then the formal agenda starts at quarter past. However, across the street, at a

HINT:
YOU CAN NEVER BE WRONG BY ASSUMING THAT 10 O'CLOCK MEANS 10 O'CLOCK.

different company, the meeting always starts promptly at 10. Coming in at 10:10 is considered rude.

2. FIGURE OUT THE PLAYERS: PLOT THE POWER.

All people are not given equal power. Identify the key players. Within any company, some people are more highly respected. Even within a given title or position, power, authority and influence will range greatly. Over time, each person has developed a reputation within the system. To ascertain someone's power or reputation:

- Be aware of words used to describe a given person.
- Watch who gets the high-profile assignments.
- Observe people's non-verbal reactions to a person's name.
- See whom leadership taps to get opinions.
- Pay attention to who gets promotions and who has not moved up.

3. FIGURE OUT THE VALUES: COMPANIES AND PEOPLE TELL YOU WHAT MATTERS TO THEM.

Pay attention to conversations: What seems to be important to the company? What matters to the people? Identify what topics come up multiple times.

- "It is all about results."
- "People matter here."
- "I went to Northwestern."
- "Hit your numbers; it's the only true measure."
- "We go above and beyond to take care of the customer."
- "I make sure I have job security."
- "The best and the brightest work here."
- "I was the top producer last year."
- "Management does not understand."
- "The president and I were talking…"

4. UNDERSTAND THE REASONS BEHIND DECISIONS.

Look for patterns within the organization. Learn about the company's history and how different people know one another. Actively try to understand the reasons behind decisions.

5. STUDY YOUR WORKPLACE: A CHECKLIST.

In each category below, there are unwritten rules or norms. Going down the list, which rules or expectations do you already know for your workplace?

For those that are not clear, start paying attention and see if you can learn the answers quickly.

To discern the unwritten rules at your company, department or role, ask the following questions:

GOALS

- How will success be judged?
- What are your targets?
- What measures will be used?

TIME

- How fast are you expected to return emails?
- What is the expected turn-around time for requests?
- How many hours are your peers working weekly?
- What kinds of hours do people work on nights and weekends?
- How much flexibility is available in start and end times?
- What time do people start and end work?
- How much time do people take for lunch and breaks?

COMMUNICATION

- What are the preferred methods of communication (text, email, IM, other)?
- Do people use voicemail?
- What collaboration tools are people using?

VACATIONS

- Do people take their vacation time?
- Are people expected to check in during vacations?
- How much do people "unplug" on vacation?

CULTURE

- How formal or informal is the environment?
- How freely is information shared?
- What are the company's current top priorities?
- How are customers treated?
- How does the company spend money?

PEOPLE

- What departments do you need to work well with?
  What is the current relationship?
- Which people, departments or functions are held in high esteem?
- Within the company, who are the most respected leaders?

WORK-LIFE INTEGRATION

- What are the policies and practices about working remotely?
- What is the openness to leaving work for personal commitments?

DRESS

- What is appropriate work attire for this workplace?
- What do the people in power wear?

LEARNING THE UNWRITTEN RULES

ORGANIZATION

What are the company's current top priorities?

_____

_____

_____

How are employees treated?

_____

_____

_____

How are customers treated?

_____

_____

_____

What are the key traits of the environment?

_____

_____

_____

What are the written and unwritten values?

_____

_____

_____

GOALS

How will your success be measured?

_____

_____

_____

What are your targets?

_____

_____

_____

PEOPLE

What people hold the most power?

_____

_____

_____

Which departments or functions are held in high esteem?

_____

_____

_____

WORK/LIFE INTEGRATION

What policies and practices are in place to support work-life integration?

_____

_____

_____

TIME

How many hours are your peers working weekly?

_____

_____

What kinds of hours do people work on nights and weekends?

_____

_____

How much flexibility is available in start and end times?

_____

_____

What time do people start and end work?

_____

_____

How much time do people take for lunch and breaks?

_____

_____

COMMUNICATION

What is the preferred means of communication (text, IM, email, or other)?

_____

_____

What collaboration tools are people using?

_____

_____

_____

VACATIONS

How fully do people use their vacation time?

_____

_____

_____

How much are people expected to check in during vacations?

_____

_____

_____

DRESS

What is appropriate work attire for this workplace?

_____

_____

_____

What do the people in power wear?

_____

_____

_____

UNWRITTEN RULES

What other unwritten rules are in place?

_____

_____

_____

_____

Chapter Two

WHAT YOUR BOSS WANTS YOU TO KNOW

The unwritten rules of working.

6. IT'S ABOUT RESULTS.

- The company did not hire you to fulfill you.
- The company did not hire you to make you happy.
- The company did not promise you a promotion.
- The company hired you because they had a job that needed to be done and they thought you would do it well.

Your job is to help the company. The company is more worried about its success than it is yours. The company may support your work-life balance, but only if the job still gets done. The company does care about you, but it cares about the business first. If you are going to be successful, it will be because you do the job well.

7. OWN YOUR CAREER.

It is your job to think through what you need to be successful and to make sure you get it. This may include asking for feedback, seeking new opportunities and surfacing issues. At the end of the day, your boss should help and guide you, but it is your job to take the lead.

HINT:
DO NOT ASSUME PEOPLE KNOW WHAT YOU WANT. ASK FOR WHAT YOU NEED.

8. KEEP YOUR COMMITMENTS.

Remember the deadlines you agree to; someone else will.

Let's say you promise something by Friday. You forget, and the deadline passes. When you promised something by a given date, someone is counting on you and that date. Letting it go will only hurt you, your relationships and the ones who are counting on you. You may end up looking forgetful or not committed to the project, the person or the company.

If you misjudge how much time something will take, or start on a project late, make the extra effort to get it done. Whenever possible, stay later, come in earlier and get it done by the deadline. If it is truly impossible for you to complete as you committed, ask for help and still get it done on time. If you cannot, go to the person early, acknowledge that you are not hitting the deadline and have a plan on how and when you will get it done.

9. YOUR LACK OF PLANNING IS NOT MY EMERGENCY.

Everyone has deadlines and deliverables. It is up to everyone to plan his or her work and make reasonable requests when working with others. If you forgot to ask for something or neglected to allot enough time to deliver on a commitment, do not expect others to jump through hoops to fix your error.

———

THE COMPANY DOES CARE ABOUT YOU,
BUT IT CARES ABOUT THE BUSINESS FIRST.
IF YOU ARE GOING TO BE SUCCESSFUL,
IT WILL BE BECAUSE YOU DO
THE JOB WELL.

10. BE ON TIME.

Get to work on time.

> Get to meetings on time.
> Get to appointments on time.
> It shows that you respect others' time.
> It shows that you can manage yourself.
> It keeps you and others on schedule.

Excuses get old quickly. Coming in out of breath, disorganized, late and blaming it on traffic or others only works a few times.

11. USE WORK TIME FOR WORK.

Limit your personal phone calls at work. The company is not paying you to shop online, check your social media, or stay connected with your friends. The company is paying you to use your work time to work.

12. SICK DAYS ARE FOR SICKNESS.

Sick days are to be used if you are sick, not if you are sick of work. Using them up too quickly can spell trouble if you get ill later in the year.

On the other hand, no one wants to get sick because you gave him or her your illness. If you have a fever, the flu or are not able to work effectively, stay home.

13. SPEND THE COMPANY'S MONEY CAREFULLY AND WISELY.

Read and heed the company expense policy. Ask for an explanation if needed. It is far better to get clarification than to violate the policy.

Don't spend the company's money with abandon. Ordering lobster every time you are out on the company tab could make you look naïve and greedy. Be careful, be conscientious and be cautious. Spend the money as if it is your own.

ORDERING LOBSTER EVERY TIME YOU
ARE OUT ON THE COMPANY TAB COULD
MAKE YOU LOOK NAÏVE AND GREEDY.
BE CAREFUL, BE CONSCIENTIOUS AND BE
CAUTIOUS. SPEND THE MONEY AS IF
IT IS YOUR OWN.

---

14. YOU ARE NOT ALWAYS RIGHT.

You may think you are the smartest person in the room. You may think you have a better way. However, not everyone wants your opinions. Don't criticize if you don't have:

- All the facts
- The background
- The rationale
- The relationships

Look for the why. Beware of critiquing what you may not understand.

15. APOLOGIZE WHEN YOU ARE WRONG.

- If you are late, apologize.
- If you cancel last minute, apologize.
- If you were wrong, acknowledge it and apologize.

16. YOU CANNOT *NOT* COMMUNICATE.

You're always communicating. You are sending messages about who you are and what you stand for all day long. People may be watching and noticing the things you do. Ask yourself:

- What messages do I send?

- What do I talk about most?
- What do I focus on?
- How does my work effort compare to others?
- Am I the first one to volunteer and pitch in or the last?
- Am I supportive or complaining?
- Am I positive or negative?

We all have choices about how to act. Be aware of your actions and make choices that will have your desired long-term impact.

HELPING OR HINDERING?

Reflect on the messages you send.
Determine if they are helping or hindering you.

~~~~~~~~~

Overall, what are the major themes of my communication?

_____

_____

_____

_____

What do I focus on? (People, Results, etc.,)   ❏ HELP ❏ HINDER

_____

How does my work quality compare to others?   ❏ HELP ❏ HINDER

_____

Do I produce more or less work?   ❏ HELP ❏ HINDER

_____

Do I work shorter or longer hours?   ❏ HELP ❏ HINDER

_____

How does the quality of my output compare with others?   ❏ HELP ❏ HINDER

_____

_____

Am I the first one to volunteer and pitch in or the last? ❏ HELP ❏ HINDER

_____

_____

Am I supportive or complaining? ❏ HELP ❏ HINDER

_____

_____

Am I positive or negative? ❏ HELP ❏ HINDER

_____

_____

What is the overall pattern behind the answers?

_____

_____

_____

What changes would be helpful?

_____

_____

_____

What are the needed actions and next steps?

_____

_____

_____

_____

Chapter Three

WHAT YOUR COLLEAGUES WANT YOU TO KNOW

The unwritten rules for bringing your best self to work.

17. WORK IS NOT YOUR THERAPY.

You may hate your mother. You may despise your ex-spouse. Your roommate may drive you crazy. Work is for work, not therapy. At one time, you selected your ex-spouse and your roommate; complaining about them could reflect poorly on you. Be cautious about using excessive work time to explore your newest relationship issues, life questions and frustrations. Work out your issues outside of work.

18. BRING THE SUNSHINE.

Daily, you choose how you present yourself at work. People prefer sunshine to rain. Bring the sunshine.

19. PLAY NICE IN THE SANDBOX.

Build relationships with your coworkers.

Greet people.
Say good morning.
Get to know them as people.
Pay attention to them.
Ask about their weekend.
Learn what is important to others.
Remember the names of their children and partners.
Build relationships before you need to make requests.

HINT:
DON'T ASSUME YOU KNOW HOW PEOPLE ARE CONNECTED. YOU MAY BE SURPRISED.

20. IT'S NOT ABOUT YOU.

Take a hard look at yourself. Are you making yourself the focus of the attention? Is it all about you? Are you demanding? How fully do you care for and support others? Are you respectful? Are you helpful? Are you kind?

21. BE YOUR STRONGEST CRITIC.

If you are being critical of yourself first, you will probably beat others to seeing and correcting your mistakes.

22. BE LOW MAINTENANCE.

There is often someone in the workplace that needs extraordinary amounts of time, attention and help. In the long run, this can become draining and frustrating for others. Whenever possible, take care of yourself emotionally and professionally. Depending on your work environment to provide all your support and stability might hurt you in the long run.

23. YOU LEAK.

Most of us do not hide our emotions well.
    If you are frustrated, it probably shows.
    If you are bored, it probably shows.
    If you do not respect your boss, it probably shows.
    Be aware of what you are thinking.

Your true feelings leak out through your non-verbal behavior. For some people, the pitch or pace of their voice changes. Others talk faster or slower under stress. You may have nervous mannerisms. Your tone, body language and eyes often betray your truest opinions. Be aware that you may be signaling acceptance, disdain, agreement or respect through your non-verbal communication.

Emma was frustrated with her new boss. She saw her new boss as far too inexperienced in their field and found her feedback to be fast, sharp and critical. When the two of them were in conversation, Emma's vocal tone was short, her arms were crossed, and she rarely looked her boss in the eye. While she thought she was hiding her feelings, her boss and coworkers could see her anger and disrespect. Finally, a colleague was kind enough to give her feedback on how her non-verbal behaviors were being seen and interpreted by the team. Emma realized that she no longer felt her role was a good fit and found a new job where she deeply respected her boss.

Be aware of your non-verbal communication. Put a mirror by your phone. Ask a close colleague. They might be happy to tell you about how you leak. Just be sure to do something with their input.

24. NO ONE IS BENEATH YOU.

While there are many levels within the workplace, every person needs to be treated well. All people count. Say hello to everyone. Get to know the housekeeper's name and use it. Treat your assistant with respect. Be supportive of others. Treating others as beneath you is wrong, inappropriate and can hurt your reputation and your image.

25. IT'S A SMALL, SMALL WORLD.

Many times, people have relatives and friends within the walls of a given organization. At one company of 1000 employees, there were 200 family relationships. Remember that you can't know all the connections and friendships. Be especially careful when starting a new job since you do not know the key relationships. You may not know who is related to another person.

Noah was not afraid to tell people what he thought. Yet, he discovered, a little too late, that the person he had been complaining about was his cube mate's sister-in-law. He apologized, but the damage was already done.

Leah is a librarian at a junior high school and her brother is the principal. Since they have different last names, people had no idea when they were complaining about the principal that he and Leah were related.

PLAY NICE IN THE SANDBOX

IDENTIFY FIVE KEY COLLEAGUES.
(BOSS, PEERS, AND KEY RELATIONSHIPS)

SPOUSE, PARTNER, KIDS,
AND PET'S NAMES

LIST THREE THINGS YOU KNOW ABOUT THEIR WORK, LIFE, OR HOBBIES	HOW CAN YOU PARTNER WITH THIS PERSON AND ADD VALUE?

Chapter Four

HELP FOR GETTING HIRED

The unwritten rules for landing the job.

26. YOUR ONLINE PRESENCE COUNTS.

Many recruiters will find you on LinkedIn first. Utilize your profile to show your skills and expertise. Look carefully at your social media. You may need to clean up your online presence before you start actively interviewing.

27. YOUR RESUME HELPS GET YOU IN THE DOOR. DON'T LIE. NO TYPOS.

Your resume and your interview answers need to be 100 percent honest.

Every word of your resume needs to be spelled correctly. No typos.

Your resume needs to show your accomplishments and work history. When possible, give details that demonstrate your competence and numbers that impress. For the interview, bring a resume for yourself and one for each person you are scheduled to meet.

> **A CASE IN POINT** Ben's role included running a conference. In his resume, he listed it as one of his duties: "Conference Manager." However, after talking to a mentor, he realized he needed to give more detail. He added, "Conference Manager: Lead for international three-day conference with more than 1,000 attendees. Oversight for marketing, faculty, event planning, logistics, speaker travel and $250,000 budget. Attendee satisfaction was 4.8 out of 5.0 and 82% of attendees returned to the conference."

28. EVERY CONTACT WITH THE COMPANY MATTERS.

When interviewing, every interaction is a chance to make a positive or negative impression. Return calls promptly. Be polite to everyone. Shake hands firmly and look people in the eye. A candidate that treats the support staff negatively is telegraphing strong signals of who they are and what kind of employee they will become. The receptionist or administrative assistant is often tapped for their opinion. Many times, interviewees show a different, less professional or unkind side of themselves to the support staff. Be nice.

29. DO YOUR COMPANY HOMEWORK.

Visit the company's website. Understand what the company does. Read the recent press releases. Know the CEO's name. Be aware if the business is growing or shrinking. Know what countries they do business in.

 Jackson was interviewing a candidate and asked him what he knew about the company. When the candidate only mentioned things that had been mentioned in the interview, Jackson realized the candidate had not taken time to learn about the company. He saw it as an indication of a lack of initiative and interest in the job. He decided to move forth with different candidates.

30. KNOW YOUR DIAMONDS.

In preparation for the interview, be prepared with ten "diamonds"—shining

---

EVERY INTERACTION IS A CHANCE TO MAKE A POSITIVE OR NEGATIVE IMPRESSION. RETURN CALLS PROMPTLY. BE POLITE TO EVERYONE. SHAKE HANDS FIRMLY AND LOOK PEOPLE IN THE EYE.

examples of your previous work— that the interviewer should know about.

31. DO YOUR INTERVIEW HOMEWORK.

Request your interview schedule from the recruiter. Google each name and learn something about each person who will be interviewing you.

Google the top ten interview questions. Practice your answers and try to keep them to three or four sentences. Consider asking a friend to do a practice interview with you. For example, some of the classic interview questions are:

- Tell me a little bit about yourself.

- What are your strengths and weaknesses?

- What interests you about this job?

- What would your former bosses tell me about you?

- Tell me about a difficult situation at work/school and how you handled it.

- What have you been learning lately?

- Tell me about a team project in which you were a member and how you worked with others.

- Tell me about a problem you solved while working with others.

Have your answers ready. Fumbling will not help you get the job.

32. BE EARLY.

Never be late to the interview. Period. No excuses.

Leave yourself an extra hour to get lost, find parking or get stuck in traffic. Do the commute the weekend or the day before the interview.

The way you behave during the interview process sends strong messages about how you will act once hired.

If you are late, it sends messages that:

- You don't organize your time well.

- You did not prepare properly.

- You do not respect others' time.

A CASE IN POINT Ericca was bringing in two candidates for her open role. Both got lost on the way to the company. The first candidate showed up 15 minutes late and apologized, saying she had gotten lost. The second candidate called a half hour early, saying she was lost and asking for help in finding her way to the campus. The second candidate started out 20 yards ahead simply because she was willing to call early.

33. DRESS WELL FOR THE INTERVIEW.

Although many companies have gone to a casual or business casual environment, you need to dress well for an interview. In many places, proper protocol says that you should still wear a suit for an interview. If the place you are interviewing wears sweatshirts and jeans, dress casually but professionally. The rule is to dress one step above the company norm.

HINT:
IF YOU ARE NOT SURE OF THE COMPANY DRESS CODE, ASK THE RECRUITER OR THE SCHEDULER.

34. NO SLAMMING YOUR PAST COMPANY, BOSS, OR CO-WORKERS.

Being negative about your past jobs, bosses or co-workers can hurt you. Instead, positively explain why you are looking for a new opportunity.

35. DECIDE IF IT IS THE RIGHT PLACE FOR YOU BEFORE YOU ACCEPT THE JOB, NOT AFTER.

An interview process in not a one-way street. While the company is interviewing you, you also need to interview the company. The interview is a time for you to assess if you would like the environment, the people and the expectations. Interview the company to make sure it fits.

In your interviews, ask questions such as:

- What traits are most often found among people who are successful here?
- What will be my key job responsibilities?
- How will my success be measured?
- What is it like to work here?

AN INTERVIEW PROCESS IN NOT A ONE-WAY STREET. WHILE THE COMPANY IS INTERVIEWING YOU, YOU ALSO NEED TO INTERVIEW THE COMPANY.

- Would you please describe a typical day?
- What hint would you give to someone considering coming here?
- What kinds of metrics are used to judge people and projects?
- What is your internal promotion rate? Among men? Among women?
- How much travel will this job entail?
- What are the normal hours you work?
- What are the expectations for working weekends?

Meet as many of your coworkers prior to accepting as possible. If possible, talk to others who have worked there or currently work there who are not on the interview list. Make small talk to others in elevators or in reception to learn more. Be friendly and ask, "I'm interviewing, what should I know about your company?"

36. DON'T TALK MONEY ON THE FIRST INTERVIEW.

You don't talk about marriage on a first date and you should not talk money on the first round of interviews. Do not ask what the role pays. Do not ask about holidays and benefits. Those conversations come once they offer you the job. Asking too soon makes you look as if you are more interested in the pay than the job.

However, you also need to be ready to discuss money when it's time.

There are huge variations in pay for the same work. Some companies pay options. Others pay bonuses. Others pay signing bonuses. The more research you do, the better prepared you are to negotiate well. If possible, do benchmarking before the interview to know what you are worth in the marketplace. Ask friends, research online and look for similar positions.

When they ask you about your salary, turn the question and ask them, "What is the range for this job?" You may be asked, "What are you making?" or "What are you looking to make?" To bypass the question, you could answer by saying, "For this job, I am looking to be paid $_____."

37. SEND THANK YOU NOTES.

A letter acknowledging an interview will still earn points. For many organizations, a thank you note is still considered proper interviewing etiquette. Many people send a follow-up email; consider setting yourself apart by sending a hand-written note.

THE INTERVIEW PREP

For each interview, know the answers to the following questions. These answers should be found on the company website and on the internet. Company financials for public companies are a part of the company's annual report which will be on their website under Investor Relations.

Company

President's name

Is the company growing or shrinking?

What countries do they operate in?

How many people work for the company?

TEN DIAMONDS

Identify ten examples that you would like to share during the interview. Make sure that the examples are concise, descriptive and demonstrate the skills needed for the role. How did it help the company? What was the impact? What measures or data do you have? What skills does this demonstrate?

1.

2.

3. _____

_____

_____

4. _____

_____

_____

5. _____

_____

_____

6. _____

_____

_____

7. _____

_____

_____

8. _____

_____

_____

9. _____

_____

_____

10. _____

_____

_____

Chapter Five

FIGURE IT OUT

The unwritten rules for starting well.

38. LISTEN BEFORE YOU TRY TO CHANGE THE WORLD.

Before you start telling people what you think, make sure you spend enough time listening and learning. Giving your opinion too soon without knowing the context and background can hurt how you are seen.

Samantha entered the organization with five years of experience. She was talkative and free with her opinions about everything— world politics, parenting and how every other department should be working. However, she did not have the position, authority or credibility for people to want her input. Two things happened: 1) Her ideas fell on deaf ears and 2) People were offended at her forthright opinions.

On the other hand, Natalie joined the firm and paid close attention. She jumped in on issues where she had expertise, yet watched and listened in areas that were new to her. People learned quickly that when Natalie spoke, she shared valuable information. She quickly gained a reputation for being a solid contributor.

39. EARN THE RIGHT TO BE HEARD.

We value the opinions of people we know and trust. We are usually not interested in the opinions of people who do not have history with us. If you want to give input and feedback, ask yourself, "Have I earned the right to be heard?"

A CASE IN POINT After a meeting, Tyler walked up to Zoe and asked her if he could give her some feedback. She said yes, and he promptly told her how she needed to be more assertive in meetings and state her opinions more strongly. Zoe thanked him and walked away.

While she was grateful for the feedback, it seemed premature. She had only been in a few meetings with Tyler and had never had a private conversation with him. In the meetings that he was referring to, she had a minor role and was in the meetings to learn rather than to take a strong lead. To learn more, Zoe went to Hannah, a trusted peer. She shared Tyler's feedback and asked for Hannah's honest perspective. Hannah gave her insight on how she saw Zoe's meeting behavior. They talked through potential changes and actions. Zoe had a deeper and better conversation with Hannah because they had already built a relationship of trust.

People want feedback from those that have their best interest at heart. Giving too much input when you may not know the people, or the situation, can hurt the relationship and your reputation.

40. YOU FIND WHAT YOU LOOK FOR. LOOK FOR THE POSITIVE FIRST.

In work, look for the things you like. If you walk in looking for the things you don't like, you will always find them. Marriage, jobs and family will always have a plethora of things to like and dislike.

41. WORK ON YOUR REPUTATION BEFORE YOU WORK ON YOUR TAN.

In some organizations, one of the unwritten rules is that being in a new job includes putting in some time before you take time off.

Taking too much vacation before you have earned a positive reputation can lead people to believe you are not putting enough effort into your work.

HINT:
IF STARTING A NEW JOB, VACATION BEFORE YOU START AND PUSH YOUR START TIME BACK.

42. START FAST ON THE RESULTS AND SLOW ON OVER-SHARING.

Be cautious in baring your soul. People don't want to know too much too soon. Some people, to create a positive image, talk too much about what they have done, who they know, and what they think. Guard against sharing too much information that is not needed or being requested.

HINT:
SHARE MINIMALLY AS YOU BEGIN YOUR WORK RELATIONSHIPS. TAKING THE PERSONAL RELATIONSHIPS SLOWLY CAN'T HURT YOU.

A CASE IN POINT Kendra was a new employee. At meetings she would make sure to tell people, "Oh, this is like what we did at my last job. We ran this program that won an award. You should do the same thing here." When she wasn't discussing her last job, she was talking about her cat, her boyfriend and her roommate. People knew too much about her personal life before they knew enough about her business capabilities.

43. YOUR ACRONYMS ARE SHOWING.

One organization has a 30-page glossary to explain the company's many internal terms.

In your organization, be aware of the need to learn the acronyms. When new people or outsiders are present, be cautious of using too much slang or too many acronyms. If there are new people present, explain the acronyms to them. If you are new and do not understand, write them down and ask a trusted colleague to explain.

STARTING WELL

In your new role, what are the five most important relationships that you need to have? How do you need to partner with these five people?

1. _____

2. _____

3. _____

4. _____

5. _____

To be successful in your new role, what are five early successes that you could have?

1. _____

2. _____

3. _____

4. _____

5. _____

What are five things you need to learn in order to be successful in your new role?

1. _____

2. _____

3. _____

4. _____

5. _____

MANAGING YOUR MANAGER

The unwritten rules for working with your boss.

44. FIND OUT HOW YOUR BOSS WORKS BEST.

Take efforts to understand how to work well with your boss. Find out:

- What are your boss's top priorities?
- Would your boss prefer to get information verbally or in writing?
- Does your boss want a phone call? Text? IM? Email?
- What does your boss most need and want from you?
- Should you go directly to your boss or go through an assistant?
- When does your boss want to be included?
- What decisions can you make on your own?
- Does your boss prefer:
  - High detail or minimal information?
  - To make decisions quickly or over time with great deliberation?
  - To see what you are working on or prefer to be left alone unless a problem arises?

Answering these questions will help you build a better, more effective working relationship with your boss.

45. THE BEST SURPRISE IS NO SURPRISE.

Mistakes happen. Things come up unexpectedly. Tell your boss and others who need to know what occurred before they find out in other ways. If your boss is going to hear about a problem, make sure you communicate about it first. Make her smart by keeping her informed.

> **A CASE IN POINT** Isabel stumbled badly during an important presentation. Her boss was not present but one of his close colleagues was there. Isabel decided her best option was to tell her boss before anyone else did. She found time on his calendar the same day and gave him the update. She also shared what she had learned and would do differently next time. Her boss saw her admission as a sign of maturity and was pleased to see Isabel take responsibility for the problem.

To share a potential problem with your boss, prepare for the discussion.

- Identify the reasons you believe it was a problem.
- Share what you have already done to contain the damage.
- Explain what you will do to prevent similar problems in the future.
- Share what you have learned.

46. YOUR BOSS IS NOT YOUR MOTHER.

Your boss has many other priorities besides you. Use your boss's time when you need direction, input or guidance on your work. Get your emotional needs met elsewhere.

47. YOUR BOSS IS NOT THE ENEMY.

Seeing your boss as the enemy will make life miserable for you both. And, since your boss has more positional power, you are likely to lose. Figure out how to partner with your boss. Ask her what she needs and deliver.

Along the same lines, complaining about your boss to your peers or your colleagues is bad behavior. If you have problems with your boss, talk to your boss first. If things do not get better, talk to Human Resources.

48. ALIGN YOUR ACTIONS WITH YOUR BOSS'S PRIORITIES. DELIVER RESULTS.

Get clear expectations from your boss. Align on your responsibilities, targets, goals and measures of success. Then, align your actions to the goals and deliver results consistently.

If you continue to get new goals and targets, re-prioritize. If you are unsure of the priorities, ask your boss.

49. MAKE YOUR BOSS SMARTER.

You and your boss touch different parts of the organization. Share key information that you hear. Keep your boss informed about things that people may mention to him. Share articles with your boss, if appropriate. If something is brewing, give him a heads-up. If you know about something that people are going to share with your boss, good or bad, keep your boss informed.

50. USE YOUR TIME WITH YOUR BOSS WELL.

Set up weekly or bi-monthly meetings with your boss. Use the time to update your boss, align on priorities, ask key questions and surface upcoming challenges. Be prepared for meetings by creating an agenda and bringing any related paperwork. Make meeting times worthwhile.

Do not assume that your boss has total recall. Help your boss recall crucial conversations. If you mention something in passing in the hall, follow it up with a reminder email. Send information ahead of the meeting so that your boss has a chance to review it.

If you have multiple issues and questions, try to bundle them together rather than leaving multiple emails or messages.

51. IF YOU ARE GOING TO SURFACE PROBLEMS, SURFACE SOLUTIONS.

Anyone can find a problem. No boss wants you to walk in, lay a problem at his or her feet, and depart. Instead, bring the problem, identify three

FEEDBACK IS GOOD FOR YOU. . . MOST PEOPLE ONLY GIVE FEEDBACK WHEN THEY MUST. THEREFORE, IT IS PROBABLY VERY IMPORTANT INFORMATION FOR YOU TO ADDRESS.

---

potential solutions and list the pros and cons of each. Know your recommendation.

Valued employees find ways to solve the identified issues. As one leader says, "No whining without offering solutions."

John was a natural at identifying problems. He would come to his boss's office with charts identifying the issues that he thought his boss, Mia, should be addressing. However, he rarely came in with solutions. Mia would ask him for options and he would fumble or answer "that was not part of his responsibilities." Mia became frustrated at John's capacity for seeing problems, but his hesitancy to take initiative to create potential answers or to jump in to fix things on his own.

Finally, she told him, "I think you only understand half of your job. I will help you to sort through answers, and there are problems that are mine to solve; however, many of these are well within your ability to address." John began to come with options for the issues. His reputation shifted to one who solved problems rather than one who surfaced them.

52. FEEDBACK IS A GIFT. UNWRAP IT. HEED IT.

Feedback is good for you. Don't fight it. Say thank you. Most people only give feedback when they must. Therefore, it is probably very important information for you to address.

Be willing and able to hear constructive criticism. You may not agree. You may not think it is fair. However, take negative feedback with dignity. If your boss (or another coworker) is giving you feedback:

- Hear the message.
- If needed, ask for examples or behaviors. Get clarification but do not argue with the feedback. It is correct in that person's point of view.
- Thank the person for their willingness to tell you.
- Depart gracefully.

- Think through the feedback thoroughly to evaluate its merit.
- Make the requested changes.
- Follow-up after a period to ask the person if they have seen improvements.

53. IT IS NOT A LEVEL PLAYING FIELD.

Your boss may like someone more than you. Your boss may have much more in common with your coworker. Your coworker may be better connected than you. You may not be part of the inner circle. Do what you can to change it. Don't whine. Move yourself forward.

54. THEY WON'T HIT YOU WITH A CROWBAR.

When something difficult needs to be said, people (especially those who veer away from confrontation) often circumvent the issue. Even though they may want to, they will not hit you with a crowbar. People often won't tell you, "You were really inappropriate in that meeting." They may soft-pedal the message.

Research supports the crowbar theory. Vital Smarts publishes an annual survey regarding crucial conversations in the workplace. They found that more than two-thirds of their respondents were avoiding a conversation with their boss, direct report or coworker. Over 90 percent reported that not having the conversation was affecting their work life.

Therefore, if your boss or coworker bothers to bring up an issue or gives you feedback, listen carefully and work on the issue.

PARTNERING WITH YOUR BOSS

Identify your boss's top three priorities:

1. _____
   _____

2. _____
   _____

3. _____
   _____

How can you support each of your boss's priorities?

1. _____
   _____

2. _____
   _____

3. _____
   _____

How does your boss prefer to get information?

_____
_____

What does your boss most need and want from you?

_____
_____
_____
_____

What three actions can you take to build your relationship with your boss?

1. _____

_____

2. _____

_____

3. _____

_____

Who strongly influences your boss?

_____

_____

_____

How should you build relationships with those influencers?

_____

_____

_____

How fully do your goals align with your boss's priorities?

_____

_____

_____

If they don't align, what actions do you need to take?

_____

_____

_____

Chapter Seven

HELP EVERYONE WIN

The unwritten rules for being a team player.

55. PLAY WITH THE WHOLE TEAM.

On every team, some people are supporting others and others seem to be looking out only for themselves. To be a good team player, actively share knowledge, share the credit when possible, talk well of others, and listen and learn from others.

 A CASE IN POINT Caleb joined his current company and immediately started to act the same way he had in his previous job. With his new colleagues, he bragged about himself, ignored others' contributions, and rarely volunteered on anything that was not high profile. People became cautious of working with him. His reputation was, "He's only out for himself."

Jana joined the same month. She asked her colleagues many questions: "What works? What do you most need from me? Tell me a little about yourself." She got in tune with her colleagues' needs and priorities. She was humble about her own contributions but was always sure to recognize and appreciate others' work. In a few short months, it became apparent that Jana was a positive addition to committees and meetings. People appreciated her ability to listen, deliver and support the team.

It does not pay to only be out for yourself. Support projects and ideas that are not just yours. Cheer for all the team members.

56. MAKE OTHERS SHINE.

- Build on others' ideas.

IT DOES NOT PAY TO ONLY BE OUT
FOR YOURSELF. SUPPORT PROJECTS AND
IDEAS THAT ARE NOT JUST YOURS.
CHEER FOR ALL THE TEAM MEMBERS.

———

- Watch how much air-time you take in meetings.
- Do not always be the first one to answer or the one who talks the most.
- View your colleagues as partners rather than competitors. Being overly competitive will hurt you if you are winning at the expense of your colleagues.

 When Colin went to meetings, he seemed to be vying for attention and affirmation. He would interrupt or jump into the conversation quickly, using such statements as, "Well, I think we should..." Grete, on the other hand, built on people's points, affirming their value before stating her own opinion. She would wait to let someone finish and then say things like, "I agree with that and I also think..." or "He makes a good point, I also would like to see us..." Grete was generally seen as more collaborative than competitive and easier to partner with than Colin.

57. YOU CAN'T FIGHT EVERY BATTLE.

Know when to die on the sword and when to back down. Being a team player means that there are many times when you need to collaborate, to give in and to move on.

Hold firm on the moral or legal questions. However, if it is a matter of opinion, everyone else agrees and it doesn't really matter in the long run, give in.

58. COOL OFF FIRST.

Many hours are spent at work. People will get on your nerves. You will feel insulted. People will get assignments, raises or promotions you thought you deserved. You will get hurt and you will get angry; it's what you do with your anger and hurt that's important.

Do not confront or storm out of a meeting when you are in shock or angry. Breathe deeply. Count to ten or to ten thousand. Take a walk. Get through the day and go home.

Get perspective. Call a trusted colleague, preferably outside of your organization. Share the facts and ask for advice. Give the situation a week; most problems are much smaller one week later. See if you need to have a conversation or to move forward.

Liam sat in a department meeting and nearly exploded when he heard his boss say, "Kevin will be in charge of the National Conference." Although it wasn't formally on Liam's job description, he had run conferences at his last job and figured that this prestigious assignment would be given to him. However, he knew Kevin also had previous experience. Although it felt impossible, Liam sat quietly and did not surface the issue.

A few days later he approached his boss and asked what his own role should be on the conference. Liam walked away with his ego intact, his experience recognized, and his goal achieved.

59. GOSSIP WILL GET YOU.

Don't talk behind people's backs. Don't talk about your boss, your coworkers, your "difficult" department or any other group that you can name.

If there are problems, identify them. Create possible solutions. Go to the source or your boss and work to resolve them.

Gossiping will hurt you in the long run. When you say, "Well, I'm not supposed to tell you this, but...." what the listener hears is the fact that you cannot keep a secret. Therefore, you lose credibility. If you talk behind someone else's back, the listener is smart enough to figure out that sooner or later, you will do the same to them.

60. YOU YELL, YOU LOSE.

Yelling in most workplaces will give you a black mark on your reputation. Disagree but do not raise your voice. If you want to yell, excuse yourself, leave the room and take a walk.

Learn the language of appropriate disagreement. Before defending your point, be sure you understand the other person's opinion. Ask questions without sarcasm or fury so you can see from their point of view. If you disagree, be sure that you affirm their right to see it their way. Make points about the issue; do not attack the person. Back your thoughts up with facts,

NOBODY WANTS TO BE CRITICIZED,
EMBARRASSED OR DRESSED DOWN IN FRONT
OF OTHERS. IF YOU HAVE ISSUES, BRING THEM
UP TO THE PERSON IN PRIVATE.

---

history and logic. Then, ask for their view of your opinion. A dialog will get many thoughts out on the table.

61. BE HUMBLE.

- If you are the best salesperson, thank the people who support you.
- If you get a promotion, appreciate the people who help you do your work.
- Let someone else sing your praises.

62. NEVER MAKE ANYONE LOOK BAD. REVENGE IS UGLY.

Nobody wants to be criticized, embarrassed or dressed down in front of others. If you have issues, bring them up to the person in private. Know that if you embarrass someone, they will be out to embarrass you.

63. ALWAYS GIVE NEGATIVE FEEDBACK PRIVATELY.

If you have negative feedback, never tell the person in front of others. If you have issues with someone:

- First, decide if it is worth a conversation. If not, quit talking about it to anyone else. Quit thinking about it and let it go.
- If yes, prepare for the conversation. Separate the facts from your emotions and your "stories" around the issues.
- Set a time and discuss it with the person in private.

- Discuss the critical issues and come to agreement on next steps.

- If appropriate, capture your agreements in writing.

64. NEVER PULL RANK.

If you have more power and authority than others, do not bring it up. Never tell anyone, "I'm the boss." Never say, "I could fire you." We all know who the boss is and we all know the power that the boss holds. Saying it only makes you look power hungry and weak.

TEAM PLAYER REFLECTION

IDENTIFY YOUR KEY PEERS	HOW WELL DO YOU PARTNER WITH THIS TEAM MEMBER?	WHAT IS THE CURRENT STATE OF THIS RELATIONSHIP?
	☺ 😐 ☹	☺ 😐 ☹
	☺ 😐 ☹	☺ 😐 ☹
	☺ 😐 ☹	☺ 😐 ☹
	☺ 😐 ☹	☺ 😐 ☹
	☺ 😐 ☹	☺ 😐 ☹
	☺ 😐 ☹	☺ 😐 ☹
	☺ 😐 ☹	☺ 😐 ☹
	☺ 😐 ☹	☺ 😐 ☹
	☺ 😐 ☹	☺ 😐 ☹

**WHAT ACTIONS COULD YOU TAKE
TO IMPROVE YOUR INTERACTIONS
WITH THIS PEER?**

Chapter Eight

LEAVE NO TRAIL!

The unwritten email, text, and voicemail rules.

I n national parks, there are often signs that say, "Leave no trail." The concept is to leave nothing behind after you hike or camp.

This same concept can be applied to email, voicemail and text. You are leaving a data trail of messages. If you are working on a company computer, the company owns the emails. If your company is paying for your mobile phone service, they have the ability and right to search its data. Anything you say over email, text or voice is a part of the company record.

65. EMAIL IS PART OF YOUR BRAND.

You may meet people for the first time over email. Their first impressions will be based on how well you communicate your thoughts. Make sure you give yourself sufficient time to send well-constructed emails; spelling and grammatical errors reflect poorly on you. Slow down. Spell check. Proof-read. Read it through three times before sending it.

SENDING NEGATIVE FEEDBACK OVER
TEXT, VOICEMAIL OR EMAIL IS DANGEROUS.
IT IS TOO EASY TO GET MISCONSTRUED
AND TO OFFEND.

Be concise and to the point. Make specific requests. Help the reader know what to do with the message. Use the subject line to help the reader understand your intent.

Avoid forwarding emails without editing. Forwarding a string of emails without editing is frustrating for the person who must read through all the peripheral information to see your intended message. Delete unnecessary information.

66. LEAVE NO TEXT, EMAIL OR VOICEMAIL WHEN YOU ARE ANGRY.

Take your time. Wait until tomorrow. The message left in anger is written or recorded proof. Sleep on the issue. If possible, sit down and have a conversation with the person. If it is impossible to talk face-to-face, make sure that you talk voice-to-voice. Try to understand their side. Then, and only then, should you share your thoughts and frustrations.

67. TEXT, VOICEMAIL AND EMAIL ARE NOT THE PLACE TO SEND TOUGH MESSAGES.

Sending negative feedback over text, voicemail or email is dangerous. It is too easy to get misconstrued and to offend. If you have strong messages, call or see the person. Otherwise, far too much can get misinterpreted.

68. DO NOT SAY ANYTHING OVER TEXT, EMAIL OR VOICEMAIL THAT YOU WOULD NOT SAY IN PERSON.

Sometimes, people say things over text, email or voicemail that they would never have the nerve or courage to say in person. Other times, someone has not thought the message through carefully. Often, in haste, a message is sent without thinking how it might land when received. If the message is something you would not say to someone's face, stop, don't send it.

69. DO NOT DRINK AND TEXT, TYPE OR LEAVE VOICEMAILS.

Drinking and then typing or texting will not help your career trajectory. Leave no voicemails after drinking.

 After attending a late work gathering during which she drank a few glasses of wine, Nyah was wide awake. Since her email box was overflowing, she decided to respond to the messages. Wisely, she saved each draft rather than sending them. The next morning, she read through her drafts and realized her writing was sloppy. She cleaned up the emails before sending them out.

Likewise, if you must leave someone voice mail, leave it before you start the evening. What may sound fine to your ears may sound slurred to the listener who may or may not know the context. You do not need anyone at the company with a record of your slurred speech or rambling tongue. Do not hurt yourself. Wait until morning.

 Margaret was a little tipsy when she left the holiday party. At 2 a.m., she left voicemails for several people in the firm. The voicemails were a little angry, a whit weepy and totally out of line. On Monday morning, the leaders realized that several people had received a voicemail from Margaret. As a professional services firm, they were astounded and worried. If Margaret did not know these boundaries, what else did she not know? Within a short time, Margaret was no longer working at the firm.

70. SEND THE EMAIL TO THE RIGHT PERSON.

Did you hear the one about the employee who accidently sent the company's compensation information to the whole company?

Did you hear the one about the ranting email someone thought they sent to their friend that went to their boss instead?

Did you hear the one about someone sharing a highly confidential email with the wrong person?

Many of these errors occur because someone is moving too fast. Each of these happened. They are all career-limiting moves. Slow down. Check the address. Send carefully.

Chapter Nine

STOP WASTING MY TIME!

The unwritten rules of meetings.

71. GATHER YOUR ALLIES BEFORE THE ALLIES GATHER.

Have the meeting before the meeting. Some of the wisest leaders know that they gather their allies before the allies gather together.

For a given idea that you will be presenting, identify the influence leaders of the group. Prior to bringing your idea to the entire group, set up one-on-one meetings with each of the thought leaders. Share your idea. Ask for feedback. Hear their concerns. Incorporate their feedback.

Ask if they are willing to support your idea. Having the meeting before the meeting makes it more likely that you will have the needed support when you bring your idea to the large group.

72. WASTE NO ONE'S TIME. BE PREPARED.

No one wants to waste time in poorly planned or unnecessary meetings.

Before calling a meeting, ask yourself the following questions:

- Can this be handled through email or a phone call?

- What is the purpose of the meeting?

    - Sharing information?

- Making a request?

- Decision making?

■ What needs to be on the agenda? How much time is needed for each item? Create an agenda.

■ Who must be in attendance? Identify who needs to be in the room and who needs to be informed after the fact.

■ How can you minimize the time in the meeting? Is there pre-work that you can send out to allow people to come prepared for the discussion?

■ For the meeting, introduce the agenda and ask for any additions or revisions. Work the agenda. Capture action steps and agreements.

■ End the meeting when the discussion is complete. No one will ever fault you for ending a meeting early.

■ At meetings where you are presenting, bring or send electronic copies of all supporting material.

73. OBSERVE MEETING BEHAVIOR AND TAILOR YOUR BEHAVIOR ACCORDINGLY.

Different companies have different behaviors regarding meetings. There are multiple opinions on using computers or phones during meetings, starting on time and handling disagreements. Work to understand the environment.

 Michael's previous manager used his computer to take notes and was fine if everyone did the same. He also texted during meetings. However, in Michael's new role, his new boss expected everyone to stay off their computers and phones during meetings. Michael quickly realized the change and followed suit.

DIFFERENT COMPANIES HAVE DIFFERENT BEHAVIORS REGARDING MEETINGS . . . WORK TO UNDERSTAND THE ENVIRONMENT.

74. DO YOUR HOMEWORK.

Before you surface a significant change or idea, ask yourself if you have fully prepared.

- Have you done your homework?
- What are the business reasons?
- What questions might come up?
- Who is the best audience for the idea?
- Have you run it by key stakeholders to get their feedback and support?
- Where will there be receptivity or push back?
- What support is needed to make it happen?

75. STOP MEETING.

What would happen if you canceled all standing meetings? One COO did this yearly. She found that the important meetings end up being rescheduled, and the meetings that wasted her time might never happen again.

MEETING PREPARATION GUIDE

Identify an upcoming meeting that you are planning or leading.

WHAT IS THE PURPOSE OF THE MEETING?	
COULD THE PURPOSE BE ACHIEVED THROUGH EMAIL? (IS A MEETING NECESSARY?)	
WHAT KEY DECISIONS NEED TO BE MADE?	
WHAT INFORMATION SHOULD BE SENT OUT PRIOR TO THE MEETING?	
WHO MUST BE IN ATTENDANCE?	
IDENTIFY EACH TOPIC AND HOW MUCH TIME SHOULD BE ALLOTTED TO EACH.	
WHO WILL FACILITATE?	
WHO WILL BE THE TIMEKEEPER?	
WHO WILL CAPTURE KEY DECISIONS AND ACTIONS AND SEND OUT TO THE GROUP?	

Chapter Ten

YOUR MOTHER WAS RIGHT

The unwritten rules of basic etiquette.

Most of us learned some basic rules in our families of origin. Many of those rules still apply in the workplace.

76. SAY "PLEASE."

77. SAY "THANK YOU."

78. QUIT SWEARING.

79. IF YOU CAN'T SAY SOMETHING NICE ABOUT SOMEONE, DON'T SAY ANYTHING AT ALL.

80. KEEP YOUR HANDS TO YOURSELF.

81. QUIT BITING YOUR NAILS.

82. PROOF YOUR WORK.

83. DRINK RESPONSIBLY.

84. DON'T BRAG.

85. PLAY NICELY WITH OTHERS.

86. SHARE FREELY.

87. PICK UP AFTER YOURSELF.

Chapter Eleven

IT'S NOT ABOUT LUNCH

The unwritten rules for navigating business lunches.

Going out to lunch for work is not about the food. If you are asked to a business lunch as a part of an interview, they are trying to see how you handle yourself.

If you are being asked to lunch by a supplier or a vendor, the person's interest is less about you and more about landing more business with your organization.

A business lunch is about business, not lunch.

88. MIND YOUR MANNERS.

- When you sit down, put your napkin in your lap.
- Chew with your mouth closed. Do not talk while chewing.
- Take small bites. Eat quietly.
- Keep your elbows off the table.
- Wait to start eating until everyone at your table is served and the host is sitting down.
- If there are multiple forks, spoons, etc., work from the outside in. If in doubt, wait and watch which utensil others are using.

- At large tables, it can be difficult to know which glass, plate or cup belongs to you. As a rule of thumb, drinks are on your right and bread is on your left. If in doubt, let the people on your right and left make the first move.

- Pass food to the right.

89. ORDER WELL.

- Be polite and nice to the wait staff.

- Decide quickly. If needed, download the menu ahead of time so that you can order easily.

- Don't order the most expensive thing on the menu.

- Order something that is easy to eat. This is not the time to order lobster, crab claws or spaghetti.

90. YOU ASK, YOU PAY.

For example, you want to network with someone and you ask him or her for coffee. You pay.

Or, you want to get insight from a peer or a leader at your firm or another firm. You ask him or her to meet for lunch, you pay.

Let's say that one of your peers hits her five-year work anniversary and you ask them to lunch to celebrate. You ask, you pay.

 Meghan was a senior leader at her company. A colleague from another company, Matt, asked her to lunch. Matt was full of questions and used the entire lunch to learn about Meghan's cutting-edge work. At the end of the lunch, Matt suggested they split the bill. While Meghan paid half, she was perturbed. She had spent time making Matt much smarter. The lunch had been all focused on his questions and his development. Meghan felt taken for granted and her opinion of Matt went down.

91. THEY ASK, THEY PAY.

Let's say you are asked to go to lunch as part of an interview process. They ask, they pay.

Let's say you start a new job and someone asks you to lunch on the first day. Offer to pay but he or she will probably will pay for it.

If it is a celebration lunch, the company will usually pick up the tab. If it is a company dinner, the company usually picks up the tab.

If an outside vendor asks you to lunch, the vendor should be picking up the bill.

92. PAY YOUR OWN WAY.

When a group of colleagues is casually going out to eat, plan to pay your own portion of the bill. Remember to add in appetizers, drinks, tip and tax.

It's been a long week and one of your coworkers suggests that you all go out for a drink. Everyone pays for his or her own tab.

93. WHEN SOMEONE IS WORSE OFF THAN YOU, BE NICE AND PAY.

Let's say the department intern asks you to lunch. You know he is a student and making very little and you have a healthy paycheck. Pick up the tab.

Let's say a colleague from a past job was laid off and is looking for a job. He asks you to lunch. While he did ask, you are working, and he is not. Pick up the tab.

———

LET'S SAY A COLLEAGUE FROM A PAST JOB WAS LAID OFF AND IS LOOKING FOR A JOB. HE ASKS YOU TO LUNCH. WHILE HE DID ASK, YOU ARE WORKING, AND HE IS NOT. PICK UP THE TAB.

94. PAY FOR YOUR OWN CAR AND TIP FOR YOUR OWN COAT.

You may have to park or valet your car. You may check your coat. Plan to pay for those on your own. Make sure you have cash to pay for your car and to tip the attendants.

95. TIP WELL.

The people waiting on you are trying to make a living. Know how to calculate a 20 percent tip. Tip well.

Chapter Twelve

POWER AND SEX

The unwritten rules for dating at work.

96. DATING AT WORK IS A POTENTIAL LANDMINE.

Spending hours together means that you may get to know people well. You may be very attracted to someone. Before moving forward, think and act very carefully.

Making unwanted advances can cost you your job.

Even if both parties want to date, your company may have strict rules about dating coworkers and direct reports. Start by being aware of the policies. Most large companies are very clear in not allowing bosses to date direct reports. Failure to follow the company's policies could cost you your job.

97. DATING A SUPPLIER CAN BE A PROBLEM.

To protect its reputation, your company may have strict policies about dating suppliers and vendors. Dating a supplier may cause people to question if preferential treatment is occurring.

 A CASE IN POINT Rick was very attracted to one of his suppliers. However, as a rising star, he did not want to hurt his career. He went to HR and said that he wanted to date the supplier. The company made assignment changes to ensure that Rick would not be making buying decisions with this supplier. Rick saved his career and found his wife.

EVEN IF BOTH PARTIES WANT TO DATE, YOUR COMPANY MAY HAVE STRICT RULES ABOUT DATING COWORKERS AND DIRECT REPORTS. START BY BEING AWARE OF THE POLICIES.

---

98. POWER AND DATING ARE A DYNAMITE COMBINATION.

If you have a higher position than the person you are interested in, there are power dynamics at play.

Your advances may be viewed as sexual harassment. Not accepting a decline for a date and asking again and again is sexual harassment. Sexual harassment will cost you your job and your reputation.

99. BEING CRUDE CAN END YOUR CAREER.

- Your sexist jokes are not appreciated.
- Your crude sense of humor should be left at home.
- No one wants to hear about your sexual conquests.

Chapter Thirteen

YOU ARE YOUR BRAND

The unwritten rules for managing your reputation.

Years ago, the cover of a popular business magazine had two words on the cover: "Brand You!" The article went on to explain that each of us has our own brand—in other words, our reputation. Managing your brand will never take the place of results and getting things done. However, being conscious of the image you portray will help people form more positive opinions of you.

100. THERE IS NOISE ABOUT YOU.

A Harley motorcycle makes a distinctive noise. It is loud and can be heard from far away.

There is also noise about you. It might be positive, such as, "She treats everyone well. You never see her stressed." Or, it might be negative: "He is so political that he only talks to people who can further his career."

Learn the noise about you. Figure out if the noise matches how you want to be seen. If not, take actions to create new noise.

101. YOUR ACTIONS ARE YOUR BRAND. DEFINE YOUR BRAND.

Get very clear about what messages you want to be sending and match your actions to your words.

- What do you want your brand to be? Name ten words that define how you want others to see you. Hone it down to five, then ask the following questions:
    - Do your work, actions and effort represent your five words?
    - Would your colleagues say that those five words describe you clearly?

102. YOUR USE OF SOCIAL MEDIA IS A PART OF YOUR BRAND.

When a recruiter or your future boss searches for you, what do you want them to see? What do your pictures and posts say about you? Do they help or hurt your brand? What messages does your online presence send? Be aware of the way you are using social media. Consider cleaning up your trail.

103. YOUR CUBE OR DESK IS PART OF YOUR BRAND.

If you walk up to a desk scattered six inches deep with paper, what do you

---

WHEN A RECRUITER OR YOUR FUTURE BOSS SEARCHES FOR YOU, WHAT DO YOU WANT THEM TO SEE? WHAT DO YOUR PICTURES AND POSTS SAY ABOUT YOU? DO THEY HELP OR HURT YOUR BRAND?

POOR CLOTHING CHOICES CAN HINDER
PEOPLE'S IMPRESSIONS OF YOUR
CREDIBILITY AND EXPERTISE.

---

assume about the person? If you walk up to a desk with nothing on it, what message does it send?

Walk up to your desk. Look at your desk as if you have never seen it before. What is your work space communicating?

104. FIGURE OUT HOW YOU ARE BEING SEEN: READ BETWEEN THE LINES.

You are being sent messages at work. Look for the messages and read between the lines.

- Are you included or excluded from key meetings?
- Do people in power make time for you or avoid you?
- Are you getting small or large raises?
- Are you selected for important projects?
- Are you feeling supported or sidelined?

If you are receiving a lukewarm response, look for the reason. Are you not delivering on commitments? Is there a lack of alignment?

Too many times, even when the person hears the hint, they may choose to ignore it.

 A CASE IN POINT Zane knew that his boss Violet didn't feel he was contributing as much as she needed him to at his level. She frequently gave him back work asking for big changes. He was not invited to be on new project teams. At year end, she gave him a smaller raise and bonus. Yet, Zane was still surprised when his job was eliminated. While the signs were there, Zane had chosen not to read between the lines and act.

105. DON'T DAMAGE YOUR BRAND—DON'T DRAW ATTENTION TO YOUR WEAKNESSES.

We all have areas that are not our strengths. Talking about them too much does not help your brand.

106. YOUR CLOTHES ARE PART OF YOUR BRAND. EVERY WORKPLACE HAS A DRESS CODE. IT JUST MAY NOT BE WRITTEN DOWN.

Your workplace has its own unwritten rules for dress. Learn what's appropriate or professional for your environment. If you're not sure how to dress, observe what the people with the power and authority wear and modify that to work for you.

Poor clothing choices can hinder people's impressions of your credibility and expertise.

What messages are you trying to send by the way you dress?

DEFINING YOUR BRAND

Identify ten words that define how you want others to see you:

1. _____

2. _____

3. _____

4. _____

5. _____

6. _____

7. _____

8. _____

9. _____

10. _____

From the list, select the five most important words. For each, grade yourself
on how well your actions are supporting your preferred brand message.

FIVE WORDS	HOW WELL DOES YOUR WORK EFFORT AND QUALITY SUPPORT THIS WORD?	HOW DOES YOUR SOCIAL MEDIA PRESENCE SUPPORT THIS WORD?	HOW WELL DOES YOUR DESK OR WORK AREA SUPPORT THIS WORD?	DOES YOUR WORK ATTIRE EMULATE THIS WORD?
	❏ SUPPORTS ❏ DOES NOT SUPPORT	❏ SUPPORTS ❏ DOES NOT SUPPORT	❏ SUPPORTS ❏ DOES NOT SUPPORT	❏ SUPPORTS ❏ DOES NOT SUPPORT
	❏ SUPPORTS ❏ DOES NOT SUPPORT	❏ SUPPORTS ❏ DOES NOT SUPPORT	❏ SUPPORTS ❏ DOES NOT SUPPORT	❏ SUPPORTS ❏ DOES NOT SUPPORT
	❏ SUPPORTS ❏ DOES NOT SUPPORT	❏ SUPPORTS ❏ DOES NOT SUPPORT	❏ SUPPORTS ❏ DOES NOT SUPPORT	❏ SUPPORTS ❏ DOES NOT SUPPORT
	❏ SUPPORTS ❏ DOES NOT SUPPORT	❏ SUPPORTS ❏ DOES NOT SUPPORT	❏ SUPPORTS ❏ DOES NOT SUPPORT	❏ SUPPORTS ❏ DOES NOT SUPPORT
	❏ SUPPORTS ❏ DOES NOT SUPPORT	❏ SUPPORTS ❏ DOES NOT SUPPORT	❏ SUPPORTS ❏ DOES NOT SUPPORT	❏ SUPPORTS ❏ DOES NOT SUPPORT

**WHAT CHANGES NEED TO BE MADE TO BETTER DEMONSTRATE
THE DESIRED BRAND WORD?**

Chapter Fourteen

ALCOHOL IS NOT YOUR FRIEND (BUT OFFICE PARTIES ARE)

The unwritten rules for company socializing.

107. AT WORK, ALCOHOL IS NOT YOUR FRIEND.

At work, alcohol will not make you smarter, faster, or better. On the other hand, alcohol may get you fired, encourage you to do stupid things, and prompt you to talk when you should be quiet.

Know your company's attitudes and policies towards drinking.

108. COMPANY FUNCTIONS ARE MEANT TO BE ATTENDED.

Company functions are intended to encourage people to develop relationships and to deepen team bonding. They are designed to offer people time to build depth and breadth in their professional relationships. Not attending these functions on a regular basis can hurt your work reputation. If your absence is frequent, it may be interpreted that you are not committed to the organization or are not willing to put in extra time. Even if you never attend because you are working, it can hurt you never to be seen during company social events.

If there is an event that you cannot attend, talk to your boss ahead of time. Explain the reason for your absence.

109. COMPANY FUNCTIONS ARE DESIGNED TO EXPAND YOUR RELATIONSHIPS.

Company functions are an extension of work. Often, companies spend the money on dinners, outings or social events to allow employees a chance to get to know one another more fully and to foster new relationships. Staying in the corner with your usual work mates may feel comfortable, but it will not earn you points for putting the company function to good use.

110. DO YOUR HOMEWORK BEFORE SOCIAL EVENTS.

You need to be able to socialize and make new connections. If this is uncomfortable for you, create a list of ten questions to ask someone. You can always start with the basic, "How long have you worked here? What do you do?"

However, you don't want to appear naïve. Study the pictures of the senior leaders. You don't want to ask the president for his or her name.

111. EACH JOB HAS ITS OWN DRINKING RULES.

At your first company party, drink slowly and moderately. Watch everyone around you to figure out the rules.

A CASE IN POINT Sarah worked at a company that made and spent money freely. At her first work dinner, she was surprised to find the host ordering bottle after bottle of very expensive wine. She soon learned that it was very appropriate in this culture to spend money freely on alcohol.

Darcy was at her first work function with her new company. She noticed that people spent a lot of time sipping and that no one ordered a third drink.

112. GETTING DRUNK WILL NOT ENHANCE YOUR CAREER.

At most organizations, work functions are not the same as college keg parties. Being drunk and acting stupid may be forgiven but will most likely not be forgotten. In addition, being hungover at work the next day will hurt you.

In a work situation, getting drunk, acting foolish or making unedited comments can become a part of your reputation.

If you are drinking at a work function, remember that you still need to face these people tomorrow. No one ever regretted drinking too little.

113. KNOW YOUR ALCOHOL ETIQUETTE.

The host of the dinner orders the wine. If the entire table is drinking wine, do not start ordering drinks.

If you are the host or hostess, learn enough about wine to order with confidence. When in doubt, ask the waiter for recommendations. If possible, prior to the event, look at the wine list and select your choices.

Guide your choices by those around you. Usually, chugging beer and doing shots will not enhance your career.

Have a go-to drink that is easy to order.

Unless your boss is ordering it, don't order the top-shelf liquor.

IF YOU ARE DRINKING AT A WORK FUNCTION, REMEMBER THAT YOU STILL NEED TO FACE THESE PEOPLE TOMORROW. NO ONE EVER REGRETTED DRINKING TOO LITTLE.

114. KNOW HOW TO BE SEEN AND KNOW WHEN TO LEAVE.

Be strategic about how you spend your time at a company function. If helpful, plan your time and your exit.

A CASE IN POINT Cameron enjoyed company gatherings. At his company, the later it got, the heavier the drinking and rowdier the conversation became. He did not want to do shots and he also did not want to have to explain his refusal. So, Cameron made sure to show up early to events. In the early hours, he socialized with intent. He had conversations with key people early in the evening, before the alcohol was pouring too fast. By the time dinner was over, Cameron had done the rounds and made a strong appearance. Then, he quietly slipped away before the drinking games began. Everyone remembered him being at the party—and his departure was not noticed.

115. THE COMPANY SOCIAL EVENT IS NOT THE PLACE TO CORNER PEOPLE AND SHARE YOUR CONCERNS AND ISSUES.

Company events are not the place to air your grievances, give the president a piece of your mind, or to try to sell your ideas.

A CASE IN POINT Eve had a few drinks at the company dinner and approached a senior leader. She loudly shared her thoughts about the need for women to get more high-profile assignments and visibility. While her thoughts had validity, the way she delivered them hurt her reputation and her future.

Chapter Fifteen

THINK IT, BUT DON'T SAY IT

The unwritten forbidden phrases.

Remember fingernails on a chalkboard? What follows are the phrases that you should eliminate from your vocabulary. These phrases will not help you.

"IT WILL NEVER WORK. WE TRIED IT BEFORE."

For the other people sitting in the discussion, this may be old, irrelevant history. The world has changed. A better response would be to surface issues that hindered the progress in the past and work together to plan a better strategy.

Inappropriate: "We tried to implement that process two years ago and it was a big mistake. It will never work here."

Appropriate: "We tried something similar before. One of the biggest challenges was engineering's unwillingness to adopt the change. Let's spend extra effort to make sure it's not an issue this time."

"IT'S NOT IN MY JOB DESCRIPTION."

The job description is meant to be a document for hiring and for outlining one's responsibilities and duties. Every job description has a line that reads something like, "Other job duties as assigned." What you are being asked to do probably fits in that category.

Inappropriate: "You can't ask me to do that, it's not in my job description."

Appropriate: "There seem to be a lot of new expectations in my role. I would like to talk about this with you so that I am clear on the priorities of my job."

Appropriate: "Since I started, there seems to be a major shift in role expectations. Would it be appropriate to add these to my job description?"

"I DON'T HAVE TIME TO DO THAT."

Others, including your boss, may or may not know what else is on your plate or how long a given request will take. Surfacing those issues can help you have a realistic conversation about demands.

Inappropriate: "There's no way that I can get that done—I don't have time."

Appropriate: "You have asked me to complete the report by tomorrow morning. That is approximately a 6-hour task. I am willing to put in the time, but I am wondering if there is any leeway in the deadline."

Appropriate: "You want this report by tomorrow. Carl has asked me to finalize my budget by 4 p.m. and I am not sure how to juggle both deadlines. Which do you see as a higher priority?"

Appropriate: "I am feeling a need to prioritize. I want to align with your areas of focus. As I see it, you would like me to address our strategic planning documents first, the competency project second and hiring new staff third. Everything else falls after those three. Is that how you see it?"

"IT IS NOT MY FAULT."

This phrase sounds like you may not be owning an issue or your behavior. Be sure you are clear on what happened so that it will not happen again.

You are responsible for your behavior. You can blame others; however, at the end of the day, you will be measured by how well you get things done, regardless of the obstacles.

YOU ARE RESPONSIBLE FOR YOUR BEHAVIOR . . . YOU WILL BE MEASURED BY HOW WELL YOU GET THINGS DONE, REGARDLESS OF THE OBSTACLES.

———

Inappropriate: "We are way behind on this project but it's not my fault. I kept going to IT and they would not give me what I needed."

Appropriate: "I am not sure how we got so behind on this project. I kept waiting for IT to get me the data and I followed up three times. Then, I stopped without taking further action. While I was not getting the cooperation I needed, I dropped the ball by not coming to you sooner."

"I QUIT."

Never offer this. Someone may take you seriously. There are far too many stories about individuals who said this and attempted to take it back the next day or the next week. Oftentimes, the company said no.

Guard against getting yourself in a situation that allows you to lose for the long term. Take a walk. Get calm. Sleep on it. Come up with another way to discuss the issue without resorting to a strong statement that could come back to bite you.

"I WON'T BE HERE LONG."

You may want to move in two years. You may have other plans. However, saying this may cause people to take you less seriously. New assignments and jobs are given to those who are seen as committed to the company.

Chapter Sixteen

ALL THINGS COME TO AN END

The unwritten rules for losing a job.

P eople lose their job for lots of reasons. The company may outsource entire departments. In mergers and acquisitions, many roles are duplicates and the company needs less people. In times of cost cutting, companies may decide to do the work with less people. In these cases, it is often more about the company than the person.

If you lose your job due to a performance issue, your manager felt that you were not demonstrating the necessary quality or quantity of work.

Regardless, it hurts to lose a job. It feels personal. You may feel wronged or embarrassed. No matter how you feel, this is a time to exit with your dignity and respect in place. Leave graciously. You may well need your boss for a reference down the road.

116. SEVERANCE IS A GIFT. USE IT WELL.

Companies differ drastically in the amount of severance they give. Larger companies are more likely to give severance while smaller companies may give nothing.

If you receive severance, use the time to find your next job.

 A CASE IN POINT After losing his job in a downsizing, Mark received a generous severance package. He used the severance funds to take many months off and treated it as a long vacation. As the severance was running out, he panicked and started looking for a job. The severance ran out before he found a new role. Looking back, Mark said, "If I had to do it over again, I would have taken a few weeks off and then started looking immediately. I hurt myself financially by not using my time covered by severance to be looking for a new job."

117. IT NEVER HURTS TO ASK FOR MORE.

If the company offers severance, they probably have a policy about the number of weeks given based on the time the person has worked at the company. However, it never hurts to ask for more time before you exit or for more severance. The best thing that can happen is that you are told yes.

Myrna's position was being eliminated and she would soon be out of a job. Myrna went to her boss and made a case to stay on a month longer to finish up a big project. She also asked for additional severance. Since she had a very positive reputation and was still delivering strong results, the company agreed to both her requests.

118. GET A GOOD LAWYER.

If you are part of a wide restructuring, the policies will be set with very little customization per person. However, if you are asked to leave or are part of a small restructuring, it is helpful to make sure you have a good lawyer reading your agreements.

Make sure the lawyer has an extensive background in corporate law. The wrong lawyer can cost you thousands of dollars in lost benefits.

Will was offered a severance package as part of his departure from a senior role. While Will did consult a lawyer, the lawyer was not familiar with company bonuses and stock options. Years later, Will said, "I was naïve. My lawyer did not know to ask for my options and year-end bonus to be pro-rated. And, since this had never happened to me, I did not know to ask. If this ever happens to me again, I will get a lawyer who knows how to help me get every dime I earned."

119. CREATE A NEW STRUCTURE AND SCHEDULE.

Some days will be very hard. For most of us, our jobs are a huge part of our

HAVING A STRONG PROFESSIONAL NETWORK IS ALWAYS IMPORTANT. IT BECOMES EVEN MORE IMPORTANT WHEN LOOKING FOR A NEW ROLE.

---

identity. And, our jobs also fill hours each day. Being without work can be hard on one's self-image, time and finances.

More than ever, it is a time to take care of oneself and move forward with intent. Transition coaches tell their clients to create a new schedule. The new schedule should create specific times to look for a job. In addition, this is also a time to get things done that may not have been possible when working full time. Spending time with family and working on long forgotten projects can give structure and support during the difficult times of transition.

120. NETWORK.

Having a strong professional network is always important. It becomes even more important when looking for a new role. Identify everyone you know who might know of roles in your field. Reach out and ask for a time to meet over coffee. Bring your resumé. Ask about the job market, needed skills, open roles and possible job openings.

 A CASE IN POINT Alan lost his role within a large corporation. Over the years, he had developed a large professional network. He developed a spread sheet and listed everyone he knew. Methodically, he met with people and kept in touch over email. He had countless coffees and lunches making connections. While it took months, he eventually landed a new role within a very different industry that offered him challenge and more money.

121. CREATE YOUR BEST LIFE.

Losing a job, either for performance or restructuring, is a very difficult experience. On tests measuring stress, it ranks as one of the highest stress

DON'T GET LOST IN ANGER, REMORSE
OR SELF-PITY. USE YOUR DEPARTURE AS
A TIME TO REFLECT AND CREATE
YOUR NEXT CHAPTER.

inducing events. Regardless of the reasons for your departure, life must go on. However, it is also a time to reflect and make new decisions. Don't get lost in anger, remorse or self-pity. Use your departure as a time to reflect and create your next chapter.

 One group of five people were all exited from an organization at the same time. One woman went back to graduate school, one took time to care for ailing parents, one retired and the other two found new jobs. Each one used their departure as a launching pad to create a new and different career and life chapter.

Chapter Seventeen

YOU ARE NEVER FINISHED

The unwritten rules for long-term success.

122. KEEP LEARNING.

The one who keeps learning wins. Explore out what other companies are doing. Identify best practices and new ideas. Look for ways to introduce innovative concepts to meet issues and challenges. Stay current with emerging trends and technology.

If you only have a hammer, everything looks like a nail. Keep getting new tools.

> **A CASE IN POINT**
>
> When he was new, Andrew was rated as excellent in his job. Yet, as time went on, he seemed to have the same set of answers again and again. His expertise had become stale.
>
> Charlie had long tenure. He survived boss after boss and new leader after new leader because he kept re-inventing himself. He stayed current in his industry and took seminars to develop deeper business expertise. He was highly respected across the entire organization.

HINT:
YOU ARE NEVER DONE GROWING.

123. ASK WHAT YOU CONTRIBUTED TO THE PROBLEM OR ISSUE.

For many of us, it is easier to blame others. Look at your own contribution first.

Ethan's project was late. He wanted to blame the marketing department for not being responsive. However, he took a hard look at himself. He had been juggling lots of issues and the project kept falling to the bottom of the list. With the marketing department, he had extensive demands and he asked for their help late in the game. When Ethan took a self-inventory, the true reason the project was late was his own prioritization and lack of early planning.

124. ASSUME GOOD INTENTIONS.

In the bestseller *Difficult Conversations,* the authors suggest we are more likely to believe that we have good intentions and that the other side does not.

Stone, Patton and Heen write, "The error we make in the realm of intentions is simple but profound: We assume we know the intentions of others when we don't. Worse still, when we are unsure about someone's intentions, we too often decide they are bad."

Oftentimes we worry about conversations or actions that are not important. We take things personally that aren't meant to be taken personally.

Jim Perrone, founder of Perrone-Ambrose Associates, Inc., often told his team, "Much of what seems personal is not." By allowing ourselves to look for alternative meanings, we can get a fuller perspective—and realize that most people have positive intentions.

125. FIGURE IT OUT.

If there are challenges and issues impeding work and progress, you need to address the issues. If it's just a matter of difference of taste or preference or style, you may need to choose to ignore it.

126. RESOLVE BUSINESS PROBLEMS.

Before you go to your boss or your coworkers to complain about an issue,

MANY TIMES, THE ISSUES WILL NOT BE RESOLVED WITHOUT CONVERSATIONS AND NEW AGREEMENTS ON HOW TO WORK TOGETHER.

---

take steps to analyze it and take action on your own.

For a business problem:

- What, exactly, is the problem?
- How long has this problem been going on?
- How is this problem impacting the business or results?
- Are you willing to take action to change the problem?
- Do work processes, timing or standards of excellence need to be clarified?
- What solutions would you suggest?
- Whose help do you need?
- Whose buy-in and support do you need?
- What actions will you take?
- How will you know if the problem is solved?

127. IMPROVE YOUR WORK RELATIONSHIPS.

Issues with coworkers may need to be addressed. Relationships need to be navigated. Many times, the issues will not be resolved without conversations and new agreements on how to work together.

Before you go to others, conduct a diagnosis to better understand the problem. Decide if you are able to solve it by taking initiative on your own.

- What, exactly, is the problem?
- When did the problems start?
- What steps have been taken to resolve the issue?

- What discussions have you had to address the issue? How did the discussions go?

- What would it take to heal the relationship?

- Do roles and accountabilities need to be clarified?

- Do standards of work or timing need to be clarified?

- Who else needs to be involved?

- Is this issue worth your time and energy?

- What are your next steps?

- How will you know if the problem is solved?

- If your actions do not solve the problem, how will you elevate the issue?

128. BURN NO BRIDGES.

We are all connected. Through social media, you can be in touch with people you worked with years ago. Some work specialties are very small. You may run into someone you knew months or years before.

129. WHEN DEPARTING YOUR JOB, LEAVE WELL.

Say goodbye well. The way you leave a job reflects your character. Resign graciously. Give notice. Allow sufficient time for your company to transition your work. Work hard until the end and wrap up projects. Thank your boss and colleagues for their partnership and support. Leave well.

REFLECTIONS | *Chapter 17*

BUSINESS ISSUE DIAGNOSTIC

What, exactly, is the problem?

_____

_____

_____

How long has this problem been going on?

_____

_____

_____

How is this problem impacting the business or results?

_____

_____

_____

Are you willing to take action to change the problem?

_____

_____

_____

What work processes or standards need to be clarified?

_____

_____

_____

What solutions would you suggest?

_____

_____

_____

What are the pros and cons of each solution?

_____

_____

_____

Whose help do you need?

_____

_____

_____

Whose buy-in, help, or support do you need?

_____

_____

_____

What actions will you take?

_____

_____

_____

How will you know if the problem is solved?

_____

_____

_____

WORK RELATIONSHIP DIAGNOSTIC

What, exactly, is the problem?

_____

_____

_____

When did the problem start?

_____

_____

_____

What steps or discussions have been taken to resolve the issue?

_____

_____

_____

What would it take to heal the relationship?

_____

_____

_____

What roles and accountabilities need to be clarified?

_____

_____

_____

What processes, timing, or work standards need to be clarified?

_____

_____

_____

Who else needs to be involved?

_____

_____

_____

Is this issue worth your time and energy?

_____

_____

_____

What are your next steps?

_____

_____

_____

How will you know if the problem is solved?

_____

_____

_____

If your actions do not solve the problem, how will you elevate the issue?

_____

_____

_____

ACKNOWLEDGEMENTS

This book has been written over years of working, consulting, and leading within organizations. I have learned at every organization. I appreciate the bosses who taught me, the teams that supported me and the peers who made me better. Thanks to my clients and my colleagues who taught me these important lessons.

Without Dave Goetz, this book would not have been published. His guidance, friendship and support are a true treasure. Jan Day worked on early versions with me. Jill DePasquale and Rob Lewis were a huge help in editing the final version. Gary Gnidovic brought the words to life on the page.

To my friends who encouraged me and gave me feedback, you are loved and appreciated more than I can express.

Michael, you are my rock. Thank you for always being my biggest cheerleader. Cameron, thank you for always challenging me to be better. Jessica, thank you for bringing sunshine. I love you all very much.